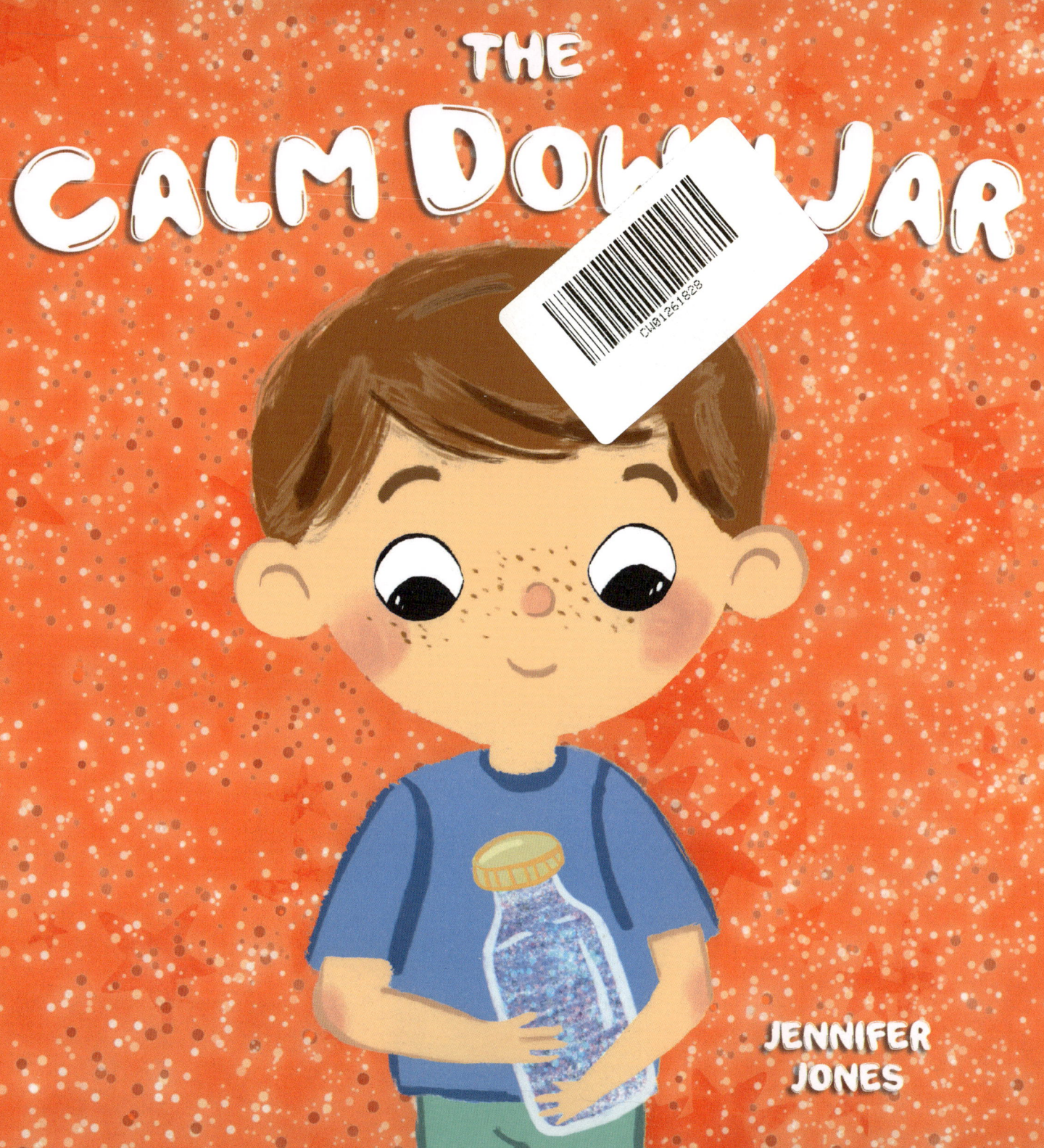

Copyright © 2022 Jennifer Jones
All copyright laws and rights reserved.
Published in the U.S.A.
For more information, email jenniferjonesbooks@gmail.com

# THE CALM DOWN JAR

JENNIFER JONES

When I'm feeling happy,
Everything is clear.
I don't worry about anything,
And there's nothing I fear.

I wear it on my face,
In my eyes and in my smile.
Being happy feels great!
I hope my happiness stays a while.

Another feeling I like is calm,
When everything is quiet and just right.
I feel easy and free-flowing,
Especially, when I drift asleep at night.

Other feelings don't feel so great,
It makes me not feel good inside.
When something is really bothering me,
My emotions are harder to hide.

My smile turns to a frown.
And my mood gets dark,
Like when my mother tells me,
It's time to leave the park.

Or when it's time for homework,
And I just want to play.
I get really upset and yell,
"I never get a say!"

In these moments, my emotions get **BIG**.
I get hot and sweaty, and turn red.
So, I try to calm myself down,
By taking deep breaths on my bed.

On top of my bedside table,
I see my **CALM DOWN JAR** sitting still.
I shake it to make the glitter cloudy,
Because that's exactly how I feel.

My mom and I made it,
To help me cope with an anxiety attack.
I watch the glitter settle down,
Which helps me to relax.

I hold the bottle in my hands,
And gently turn it upside down.
As I stare at the glitter moving,
I can turn my emotions right around.

The glitter is a lot like my feelings,
Sometimes it's settled and at rest.
When I'm feeling calm and happy,
I'm like the glitter, calm and at my best.

At times, I have big emotions,
My feelings, like the glitter, starts to swirl.
Even something small,
Can feel like it affects my entire world.

The worst is when I'm angry.
My feelings are quite a mess,
Clumps of blue and yellow flying all around,
Frantically and in stress.

The glitter spreads all around,
Just like my anger can.
It can bring others down,
Even if that's not my plan.

Once it's spread and messy.
It's hard to bring it all in.
Sometimes, it's hard to breathe,
And it worries my parents and friends.

But I've learned a special trick,
That helps me get back to calm.
I take a deep breath to feel calm again
And then I just hang on.

I count to three in my head,
One, two, three...
I exhale to breathe out,
Then, once again I feel like me.

The glitter in my **CALM DOWN JAR'S** settled,
And reaches the bottom to rest.
When my breathing and heart are steady,
That's when I feel my best.

I'm glad I have a **CALM DOWN JAR**,
It helps me to relax, you see.
So that when I'm no longer upset,
I can get back to being my favorite me!

## HOW TO MAKE YOUR CALM DOWN JAR:

You'll need the following ingredients for your very own calm down jar.

* Clean Voss Plastic Bottles
* Hot water
* Mixing Bowl (preferably one with a pouring spout to easily put it in the calm down jar)
* Whisk
* Liquid Watercolor or food coloring
* Fine Glitter

The calm down jar is made with about 20% glue, 80% water, and as much glitter as desired.

Pour glue and hot water into the mixing bowl, along with some liquid watercolor or food coloring, and glitter. Now mix with the whisk. When everything is blended, mix vigorously then pour right away into the water bottle. The last stir helps get the glitter to transfer to the water bottle instead of settling in the mixing bowl. Add a bit of hot water to the mixing bowl if there is some that is stuck.

I love to hear from my readers. Write to me at jenniferjonesbooks@gmail.com

Please visit chairsonstrike.com for the latest news and updates on future titles!

Printed in Great Britain
by Amazon